Collins

SNAP
REVISION

ALGEBRA

Edexcel GCSE Maths Higher

C000118074

EDEXCEL
GCSE MATHS
HIGHER

REVISE TRICKY
TOPICS IN A SNAP

Contents

Published by Collins
An imprint of HarperCollins*Publishers* Ltd
1 London Bridge Street
London SE1 9GF

© HarperCollins*Publishers* 2016

ISBN 9780008217891

First published 2016

10 9 8 7 6 5 4 3 2 1

Printed in Great Britain by Martins the Printers

ACKNOWLEDGEMENTS

The author and publisher are grateful to the copyright holders for permission to use quoted materials and images.

All images are © Shutterstock.com

Every effort has been made to trace copyright holders and obtain their permission for the use of copyright material. The author and publisher will gladly receive information enabling them to rectify any error or omission in subsequent editions. All facts are correct at time of going to press.

How To Use This Book

To get the most out of this revision guide, just work your way through the book in the order it is presented.

This is how it works:

Revise

Clear and concise revision notes help you get to grips with the topic

Revise

Key Points and Key Words explain the important information you need to know

Revise

A Quick Test at the end of every topic is a great way to check your understanding

Practise

Practice questions for each topic reinforce the revision content you have covered

Review

The Review section is a chance to revisit the topic to improve your recall in the exam

Basic Algebra

You must be able to:

- Use and understand algebraic notation and vocabulary
- Simplify and rearrange expressions, including those that involve algebraic fractions
- Expand and factorise expressions
- Solve linear equations.

Basic Algebra 4/19

- 'Like terms' are terms with the same variable, e.g. $3x$ and $4x$ are like terms because they both contain the variable x.
- To simplify an expression you must collect like terms.
- When moving a term from one side of an equation to the other, you must carry out the inverse operation.

> **Key Point**
>
> When simplifying expressions, remember to:
> - Use BIDMAS
> - Show your working.

Simplify $3x + 3y - 7x + y$

$4y - 4x$ ←

$3x - 7x = -4x$
$3y + y = 4y$

Simplify $9p^2 + 7p - qp + pq - p^2$ ←

$qp = pq$

$8p^2 + 7p$ ←

$9p^2 - p^2 = 8p^2$
$-qp + pq = 0$

- Substitution means replacing variables with numbers.

> **Key Point**
>
> An expression does not contain an = sign.

If $y = 4$ and $t = 6$, work out the value of $7y - 6t$

$$7y - 6t = 7 \times 4 - 6 \times 6$$
$$= 28 - 36$$
$$= -8$$

If $q = 5$, $r = 2$ and $z = -3$, work out the value of $rq + z^2$

$$rq + z^2 = 2 \times 5 + (-3)^2$$ ←
$$= 10 + 9$$
$$= 19$$

Use brackets as the minus sign is also squared.

> **Key Point**
>
> Always apply the rules:
> $- \times - = +$
> $+ \times + = +$
> $- \times + = -$
> $+ \times - = -$

- To expand or multiply out brackets, every term in the bracket is multiplied by the term outside the bracket.

Multiply out $5p(p - 2)$

$5p^2 - 10p$ ←

$5p \times p = 5p^2$
$5p \times (-2) = -10p$

Expand and simplify $4y(2y - 3) - 3y(y - 2)$

$8y^2 - 12y - 3y^2 + 6y$ ←
$= 5y^2 - 6y$

Note that $-3y \times -2 = +6y$

Factorisation 4/19

- **Factorisation** is the reverse of expanding brackets, i.e. you take out a common factor and put brackets into the expression.
- To factorise, you should look for common factors in every term.

Factorise $3x^2 - 6x$

$3x(x - 2)$

Factorise $3p^3 - 2p^2 + 8p$

$p(3p^2 - 2p + 8)$

> **Key Point**
>
> To factorise completely, always take out the highest common factor, e.g. 3 is the HCF of 3 and 6.

Linear Equations 4/19

- Equations can be used to represent real-life problems.
- The equation should be rearranged to solve the problem.

> Remember $x^2 = x \times x$

Solve $5y - 4 = 3y + 10$

$5y - 3y = 10 + 4$

$2y = 14$

$y = 7$

> Collect all the letter terms on one side.

> **Key Point**
>
> When moving a term from one side of an equation to the other, you must carry out the inverse operation.

Mary bought nine candles. She used a £3 gift voucher as part payment. The balance left to pay was £5.55.

What was the cost of one candle (c)?

$9c - 3 = 5.55$

$9c = 8.55$

$c = \frac{8.55}{9}$

$c = £0.95$ or 95p

> Use the information given to set up an equation.

> Solve to find the cost of one candle.

Algebraic Fractions 4/19

- When solving equations involving **fractions**, take extra care when rearranging and make sure you carry out the inverse operations in the correct order.

Solve $\frac{3x - 3}{4} = 7$

$3x - 3 = 28$

$3x = 31$

$x = \frac{31}{3}$

Solve $\frac{5s}{4} + 3 = 18$

$\frac{5s}{4} = 15$

$5s = 60$

$s = 12$

> Subtract 3 from both sides.

> Multiply both sides by 4.

> Divide both sides by 5.

> **Key Words**
>
> term
> variable
> expression
> equation
> inverse operation
> factorisation
> fraction

> **Quick Test**
>
> 1. Simplify $2y - 7 + 4y + 2$
> 2. Work out the value of $3p^3 - 7q$, when $p = -4$ and $q = -3$
> 3. Expand the following expression: $3t(4t - 1)$
> 4. Factorise completely $4r^3 - 2r^2$
> 5. Solve the equation $5(t + 4) = 3(6 - t)$

Factorisation and Formulae

You must be able to:

- Expand products of two or more binomials
- Factorise a quadratic expression
- Understand and use formulae
- Rearrange and change the subject of a formula.

Binomial Expansion

- A **binomial** is an **expression** that contains two terms, e.g.
  $3y^2 + 12$, $4xy - x^2$ or $5x^3 + 3x^2$
- The product of binomials is obtained when two or more
  binomials are multiplied together, e.g. $(2r + 7)(3r - 6)$
- To **expand** (or multiply out) the brackets, every term in the first
  set of brackets must be multiplied by every term in each of the
  other sets of brackets.

> **Key Point**
>
> Make sure you multiply every term inside the bracket.

> **Key Point**
>
> Take care over + and − signs.
> Remember $x^m \times x^n = x^{m+n}$

Expand $(2y + 4)(3y - 2)$

×	$2y$	$+4$
$3y$	$6y^2$	$+12y$
-2	$-4y$	-8

$6y^2 + 12y - 4y - 8$
$= 6y^2 + 8y - 8$ ← Simplify by collecting like terms.

Expand $(4z + 3)(2z - 1)(4 - z)$

×	$4z$	$+3$
$2z$	$8z^2$	$+6z$
-1	$-4z$	-3

← Multiply out the first two brackets.

×	$8z^2$	$+2z$	-3
4	$32z^2$	$+8z$	-12
$-z$	$-8z^3$	$-2z^2$	$+3z$

← Multiply the product of the first two brackets with the final bracket.

$8z^2 + 6z - 4z - 3$
$= 8z^2 + 2z - 3$

$32z^2 + 8z - 12 - 8z^3 - 2z^2 + 3z$
$= -8z^3 + 30z^2 + 11z - 12$ ← Write in descending powers of z.

Quadratic Factorisation

- An expression that contains a squared term is called **quadratic**.
- Some quadratic expressions can be written as a product of two
  binomial expressions.
- When written in factorised form, the new expression is
  equivalent to the original quadratic.
- To factorise a quadratic, you can use a table as in the expansion
  examples above:
  1. Complete the table with as much information as you can.
  2. Work out the missing terms (it may take more than one
     attempt to find the correct pair of numbers).
  3. Write out the factorised expression.

> **Key Point**
>
> Check you have factorised correctly by expanding the brackets – your expressions should be equivalent.

- If the coefficient of x^2 is **not** 1, more care must be taken.

Factorise the expression
$x^2 + 4x + 3$

×	x	+1
x	x^2	$+x$
+3	$+3x$	$+3$

The missing terms need to have a product of +3 and a sum of +4, i.e. 1 and 3.

$(x + 1)(x + 3)$

Write the expression as a product: the **first row** gives you the **first bracket** and the first column gives you the **second bracket**.

Factorise the expression
$2y^2 - 3y - 20$

×	**2y**	+5
y	$2y^2$	$+5y$
-4	$-8y$	-20

$(2y + 5)(y - 4)$

+5 and -4 is the pair that gives -3y.

Note that the coefficient of y^2 is not 1.

Possible pairs of numbers are -20 and 1; 20 and -1; 10 and -2; -10 and 2; -4 and 5; -5 and 4.

Changing the Subject of a Formula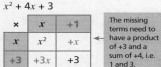

- A **formula** is a way of describing a rule or fact.
- A formula is written as an algebraic equation.
- The **subject** of a formula appears once on the left-hand side.
- To change the subject, a formula must be rearranged using **inverse operations**.

This formula can be used to change temperature in degrees Fahrenheit to temperature in degrees Celsius: $C = \frac{5}{9}(F - 32)$

In Iceland, the lowest recorded temperature on a certain day is $-20°C$. What is this temperature in degrees Fahrenheit?

$-20 = \frac{5}{9}(F - 32)$

$-180 = 5(F - 32)$

$-36 = F - 32$

$F = -4°F$

The formula must be rearranged to find the value of F.

The answer is -4 degrees Fahrenheit.

Make r the subject of the formula $P = 3(r - 1)$

$\frac{P}{3} = r - 1$

$r = \frac{P}{3} + 1$

The formula for calculating the area of a circle is $A = \pi r^2$
Make r the subject.

$\frac{A}{\pi} = r^2$

$r = \sqrt{\frac{A}{\pi}}$

π can be treated as a numerical term.

Only the positive root is needed as r is a length.

Collect all the terms containing q on one side.

Make q the subject of the formula $p + q = pq - 5$

$p + 5 = pq - q$

$p + 5 = q(p - 1)$

$q = \frac{p + 5}{p - 1}$

Take q out as a factor.

$3|19$ $v = pq$ $p - 5$
$v = p(q - 1) - 5$ ✗

Quick Test

1. $T = 30w + 20$. Work out the value of w when $T = 290$
2. Expand and simplify $(y + 4)(y - 2)$
3. Factorise $2q^2 + 7q + 3$
4. Make y the subject of the formula $\frac{x + y}{3} = 2(y - 1)$

$2c + y = 6(y - 1)$

$\frac{x + 6}{5} \neq 8y$ $y = \frac{x + 6}{5}$

$3|19$

Number Patterns and Sequences

You must be able to:

- Work out missing terms in sequences using term-to-term rules and position-to-term rules
- Recognise and use arithmetic and geometric sequences
- Work out the rule for a given pattern.

Patterns in Number 4/19

- A **sequence** is a series of shapes or numbers that follow a particular pattern or rule.
- A **term-to-term rule** links the next term in the sequence to the previous one.
- A **position-to-term rule**, also called the nth term, can be used to work out any term in the sequence.
- A **recursive** relationship is used to define further terms in a sequence, when one or more initial terms are given.

> Write down the next two terms in the following sequence.
>
> 7, 11, 15, 19, __, __
>
> The term-to-term rule is +4, so the next two terms are 23 and 27.
>
> This sequence can be expressed by the recursive relationship
> $U_{n+1} = U_n + 4$, $U_1 = 7$
>
> This states that the first term is 7.
> Therefore, U_5 (the fifth term) = $U_4 + 4 = 19 + 4 = 23$

$7 \quad U_1, \; 11 \; U_2,$
$15 \; U_3, \; 19 \, U_4$

General Rules from Given Patterns 4/19

Here is a sequence of patterns made from matchsticks:

pattern 1   pattern 2   pattern 3

a) Draw the next pattern in the sequence.

b) Write down the sequence of numbers that represents the total number of matchsticks used in each pattern and work out an expression for the position-to-term rule.

The expression for the position-to-term rule is $3n + 1$

Pattern No.	1	2	3	4	n
No. of Matchsticks	4	7	10	13	$3n + 1$

Key Point

For the first term in any sequence, $n = 1$

The nth term of a number sequence is $5n + 2$.

Write down the first five terms of the sequence.

$(5 \times 1) + 2 = 7$ ← To work out the first term, substitute $n = 1$ into the expression.

$(5 \times 2) + 2 = 12$ ←

7, 12, 17, 22, 27 ← To work out the second term, substitute $n = 2$ into the expression.

Number Sequences 4/19

Continue until $n = 5$ to produce the first five terms of the sequence.

- In an **arithmetic sequence** there is a common difference between consecutive terms, e.g.
  5, 8, 11, 14, 17 … ← The terms have a common difference of +3.

- In a **geometric sequence** each term is found by multiplying the previous term by a constant, e.g.
  20, 10, 5, 2.5, 1.25 … ← The constant (or ratio) is 0.5

The nth term of an arithmetic sequence is $4n - 1$.

a) Write down the term-to-term rule.

The sequence of numbers is 3, 7, 11, 15, 19 … ← Work out the first five terms.
The term-to-term rule is +4.

b) Marnie thinks that 50 is a number in this sequence.
Is Marnie correct? Explain your answer.

$4n - 1 = 50$, $n = 12.75$

n is not a whole number, so 50 is **not** in this sequence.
Marnie is wrong.

Here is a geometric sequence: 4, 6, 9, __, 20.25

What is the missing term?

$\frac{6}{4} = \frac{9}{6} = 1.5$ ← Divide at least two given terms by the previous term to work out the ratio.

$9 \times 1.5 = 13.5$ ← Multiply by the ratio to find the missing term.
The missing term is 13.5

Quick Test

1. Here are the first five terms of a sequence: 16, 12, 8, 4, 0 … 1) $-4, -8$ ✓
   Write down the next two terms.
2. The nth term of a sequence is $5n - 7$. 2) $-2, 43$
   Work out the 1st term and the 10th term of this sequence.
3. In the sequence below the next pattern is formed by adding another layer of tiles around the previous pattern.

Work out how many tiles will be needed for the 6th pattern.

Key Words

sequence
term-to-term rule
position-to-term rule
nth term
recursive
arithmetic sequence
geometric sequence

3) 2   8   18   32
   +6 +10   +14
   $2n + 4$ $U_{n+1} = U_n +$

Terms and Rules

4/19

You must be able to:

- Deduce and use expressions to calculate the nth term of a linear sequence
- Deduce and use expressions to calculate the nth term of a quadratic sequence
- Recognise and use sequences of triangular numbers, squares, cubes and other special sequences.

Finding the nth Term of a Linear Sequence

- A number sequence that increases or decreases by the same amount each time is called a linear sequence.
- To work out the expression for the nth term in a linear sequence, look for a pattern in the numbers.
- Using a function machine to represent a sequence of numbers can help.

The first five terms of a sequence are: 9, 12, 15, 18, 21 ...

What is the expression for the nth term of this sequence?

The term-to-term rule is +3, so the expression for the nth term starts with $3n$.

Input (n)	× 3 ($3n$)	Output
1	3	9
2	6	12
3	9	15
4	12	18
5	15	21
n	$3n$	$3n + 6$

The 'input' is the position of the term and the 'output' is the value of the term.

The difference between $3n$ and the output in each case is 6, so the expression for the nth term is **$3n + 6$**.

> **Key Point**
>
> The zero term is the term that would come before the first term in a given sequence of numbers.

- The alternative method is to work out the zero term.

The first five terms of a sequence are: 20, 16, 12, 8, 4 ...

The difference between terms is –4.

What is the expression for the nth term of this sequence?

Input	Output
0	zero term
1	20
2	16
3	12
4	8
5	4
n	nth term

The zero term is (20 + 4 =) 24

The expression for the nth term is $-4n + 24$ or $24 - 4n$.

The nth term = 'the difference' × n + the zero term

Special Sequences

- It is important to be able to recognise special sequences of numbers:
  - square numbers: 1, 4, 9, 16, 25 ...
  - cube numbers: 1, 8, 27, 64, 125 ...
  - triangular numbers: 1, 3, 6, 10, 15 ...
  - the **Fibonacci sequence**: 1, 1, 2, 3, 5, 8, 13, 21 ...

> The nth term is n^2

> The nth term is n^3

> The nth term is $\frac{n}{2}(n + 1)$

> Work out the expression for the nth term of the following
> sequence: 2, 9, 28, 65, 126 ...
> The expression for the nth term is $n^3 + 1$

> The recursive relationship can be written as $U_{n+2} = U_{n+1} + U_n$

> The cube numbers produce the sequence 1, 8, 27, 64, 125 ... This sequence of numbers is one greater than the cube numbers.

Finding the nth Term of a Quadratic Sequence

- A **quadratic sequence** contains an n^2 term as part of the expression for the nth term.
- The general form of a quadratic sequence is $an^2 + bn + c$, where a, b and c are constants.
- To find the expression for the nth term of a quadratic sequence, look to see if you can spot the pattern.
- If this doesn't work, extend the difference backwards to get the zero term ($n = 0$).

> Work out the expression for the nth term of the following
> sequence of numbers: 0, 3, 8, 15, 24, 35 ...
> $n^2 - 1$

> The numbers are one less than the square numbers.

> Work out the expression for the nth term of the following
> sequence of numbers: 4, 13, 26, 43 ...

n	0		1		2		3		4
c (nth Term)	−1		4		13		26		43
$a + b$ (First Difference)		5		9		13		17	
$2a$ (Second Difference)			4		4		4		

> Set up a difference table that extends backwards to get the term for $n = 0$.

$c = -1$
$2a = 4$, so $a = 2$ $a + b = 5$, so $b = 3$
The expression for the nth term is $2n^2 + 3n - 1$

> In the form $an^2 + bn + c$

Quick Test

1. a) Work out the expression for the nth term for the following sequence: 7, 10, 13, 16, 19 ...
   b) Work out the 50th term in this sequence.
2. Write down the next two terms in this quadratic sequence: −4, −1, 4, 11, 20, __, __
3. Write down an expression for the nth term for the following sequence of numbers: 0, 7, 26, 63, 124 ...

Key Words

linear sequence
zero term
Fibonacci sequence
quadratic sequence

4/19

Basic Algebra & Factorisation and Formulae

1. Simplify $5x - 2y + 4x + 6y$ 🔢 $9x + 4y$ [2]

2. Simplify $5 - 3z + y - 5z + 7 + 3y$ 🔢 $4y - 8z + 12$ [2]

3. Simplify $3x^2 + 3x + x^2 + 4 - x$ 🔢 $4x^2 + 2x + 4$ [2]

4. Work out the value of $3z^2 - 2q + 5$ when $z = -2$ and $q = -3$ 🔢 $12 + 6 + 5 = ph = 23$ [1]

5. Solve $4(2b - 3) = 2$ 🔢 $8b - 12 = 2$ $b = 14/8 = 7$ [2]

6. Solve $3(p + 2) = 2(p + 3)$ 🔢 $3p + 6 = 2p + 6$ $p = 0$ [2]

7. Solve $\frac{5}{2}x - \frac{1}{3} = \frac{2}{3}x + \frac{1}{2}$ 🔢 $x6$ $15x - 2 = 4x + 3$ $11x = 5$ $x = 1)$ [3]

8. Expand $6(x - 5y + 6)$ 🔢 $6x - 30y + 36$ [2]

9. Expand $6p - 4(q - 3)$ 🔢 $6p - 4q + 12$ [2]

10. Factorise completely $4xyz - 4xz$ 🔢 $4xz(y - 1)$ [2]

11. Expand and simplify $(w + 4)(w + 1)(w - 4)$ 🔢 $w^2 + 5w + 4$ [3]

$w^3 + 5w^2 + 4w$
$-4w^2 - 20w$
$w^3 + w^2 - 16w - 16$

12. Factorise $x^2 + 3x + 2$ 🔢 $(x + 2)(x + 1)$ [2]

13. Write $3(2x - 5) + 4(x + 3) - 4x$ in the form $a(bx + c)$, where a, b and c are integers. 🔢 [3]

14. Rearrange the formula to make y the subject: $x = \frac{1 - 2y}{3 + 4y}$ 🔢 [3]

$3x + 4xy = 1 - 2y$
$x(3 + 4y) = 1 - 2y$
$3x + 4xy - 1 + 2y = 0$

15. The formula for the area of a trapezium is $A = \frac{1}{2}(a + b)h$ 🔢

a) Rearrange the formula to make h the subject. $\frac{2A}{a + b} = h$ [2]

$2y(2x + 1) = 1 - 3x$
$y = \frac{1 - 3x}{2(2x + 1)}$

b) The area of a trapezium is 24cm². Work out the value of h if $a = 5$cm and $b = 7$cm. [2]

$h = \frac{48}{12}$ $\frac{24}{6} \leq M$

16. Factorise $x^2 + 5x + 6$ 🔢 $x(x+3)(x+2)12$ [2]

$y = \frac{1 - 3x}{4x + 2}$

17. $V = \sqrt{u^2 - 10p}$ 🔢

a) Work out the value of V when $u = 10$ and $p = 5$. $\sqrt{50}$ [2]

b) Rearrange the formula to make u the subject. [2]

$V^2 = u^2 - 10p$ $u \leq \sqrt{V^2 + 10p}$

13 $6x - 15 + 4x + 12 - 4x$ $6x - 3$
$3(2x - 1)$

Number Patterns and Sequences & Terms and Rules

1 Here is a sequence:

20, 16, 12, 8, 4 ...   *[handwritten: 24 − 4n]*

Write down the expression for the nth term of the sequence.   [2]

2 Work out the first five terms in the sequence with the nth term $3n - 5$.   *[handwritten: −2, 1, 4, 7, 10]* [2]

3 The first five terms of an arithmetic sequence are 14, 17, 20, 23, 26 ...

a) Write an expression for the nth term of this sequence.   *[handwritten: 11 + 3n]* [2]

b) Calculate the 100th term in this sequence.   *[handwritten: 11 + 3 × 100 = 311]* [1]

4 The population of a culture of bacteria is given by the formula:

$P = 10 \times 2^t$, where t is the time in hours.

a) What is the initial population of bacteria?   *[handwritten: 10]* [2]

b) What is the size of the population after five hours?   *[handwritten: 10 × 2^5 = 320]* [2]

c) After how many hours will the population exceed 1000?   *[handwritten: 7]* [2]

d) Is this a sensible formula to model the population? Explain your answer.   *[handwritten: No, die]* [1]

5 a) A sequence of numbers is given as 5, 8, 12, 19 ...   *[handwritten: A 30, 48]*

Write down the next two terms in the sequence.   *[handwritten: n = current, n = (n−1) + (n−2) − 1]* [2]

b) A second sequence of numbers is given as 2, 3, 2, 3, 2, 3 ...

Write down the 100th term.   *[handwritten: 3, modified Fibonacci, Help via Quora]* [1]

6 These are the first two patterns in a sequence made using matchsticks:

a) Draw the next two patterns in the sequence.   *[handwritten: 3 5 7 9]* [2]

b) Write down the rule for the number of matchsticks required for pattern number n.   *[handwritten: 2n+1]* [2]

c) Use the rule to work out how many matchsticks are required for pattern 100.   *[handwritten: 201]* [1]

7 The first five terms of a quadratic sequence are:

4, 15, 32, 55, 84 ...   *[handwritten: 3n² + 2n, 3 + b = 5, b = 2]*

Write down the expression for the nth term of this sequence.   [3]

Total Marks _____ / 25

Linear Graphs

47/19

You must be able to:

- Work with coordinates in all four quadrants
- Plot graphs of linear functions
- Work out the equation of a line through two given points or through one point with a given gradient
- Work out the gradient and y-intercept of a straight line in the form $y = mx + c$.

Drawing Linear Graphs from Points

- **Linear graphs** are straight-line graphs.
- The equation of a straight-line graph is usually given in the form $y = mx + c$, where m is the **gradient** of the line and c is the **intercept** of the y-axis.
- $y = mx + c$ is a function of x, where the input is the x-coordinate and the output is the y-coordinate.

Draw the graph of the equation $y = 2x + 5$

Use values of x from -3 to 3.

x	-3	0	3
y	-1	5	11

First, draw a table of values. Include a third value as a check.

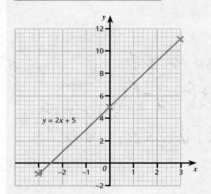

$y = 2x + 5$

2 values +
1 check
value

Drawing Graphs by Cover-Up and Gradient–Intercept Methods

- Another method that can be used to draw a graph is the cover-up method.
- This can be used for equations in the form $ax + by = c$.

New method. OR $y = -\frac{2}{3}x + 2$ ← *stick with this!*

Draw the graph of the equation $2x + 3y = 6$

$3y = 6$
$y = 2$ The y-intercept is (0, 2).

Cover up the x term and solve to find y.

$2x = 6$
$x = 3$ The x-intercept is (3, 0).

Cover up the y term and solve to find x.

- The gradient–intercept method is used for equations in the form $y = mx + c$.

Draw the line with equation $y = 4x + 2$

Find the value for y when $x = 0$.

The y-intercept is (0, 2).

The gradient is 4.

m is the gradient in the equation $y = mx + c$

Therefore, another coordinate on the line is (1, 6).

$y = 4x + 2$ $y = 4x + 1$

Gradient $= \frac{4}{1}$ so for every 1 across, go up 4.

Finding the Equation of a Line

- To find the equation of a straight line in the form $y = mx + c$, work out the gradient and y-intercept.

Key Point

$\text{Gradient} = \dfrac{\text{Change in } y}{\text{Change in } x}$

If the line slopes down from left to right, the gradient is negative.

Work out the equation of the line that joins the points (1, 20) and (4, 5).

Gradient $= \frac{15}{-3}$
$= -5$

$y = mx + c$
$y = -5x + c$
$20 = (-5 \times 1) + c$
$c = 25$

The equation of the line is $y = -5x + 25$

To work out the value of c, substitute in point (1, 20) or (4, 5).

Graphs of Quadratic Functions

Algebra

You must be able to:

- Recognise, sketch and interpret graphs of quadratic functions
- Identify and interpret roots, intercepts and turning points of quadratic functions
- Work out roots using algebraic methods
- Work out turning points.

Plotting Quadratic Graphs 4/19

- A **quadratic equation** is an equation that contains an unknown term with a power of 2, e.g. x^2.
- You can use a table of values to draw **quadratic graphs**.

Draw the graph of the function $y = 2x^2 + 1$

x	−2	−1	0	1	2	3	4
y	9	3	1	3	9	19	33

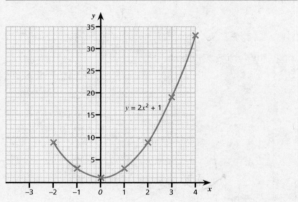

The Significant Points of a Quadratic Curve

- A sketch shows the shape and significant points on a graph, but is not an accurate drawing.
- To sketch a quadratic, work out the **roots**, the **intercept** and the **turning point**, i.e. the **maximum** or **minimum point**.
- The roots are found by solving the quadratic when $y = 0$.
- Because quadratic curves are symmetrical, the x coefficient of the turning point is halfway between the two roots.

Key Point

All quadratic graphs have a line of symmetry, which passes through the turning point.

The roots of a quadratic equation are the points where the graph crosses the x-axis. Not all quadratic curves will have roots.

Sketch the graph of equation $y = x^2 + 5x + 4$

Roots: **y-intercept:**

$x^2 + 5x + 4 = 0$ $y = 4$

$(x + 4)(x + 1) = 0$ y-intercept is (0, 4)

$x = -4$ or $x = -1$

> Substitute $x = 0$ into the equation.

> Work out the values for x when $y = 0$.

Turning Point:

$x = -4$ and $x = -1$, therefore $x = -2.5$

$y = (-2.5)^2 + (5 \times -2.5) + 4$

$= -2.25$

minimum point is (−2.5, −2.25)

(−2.5, −2.25)

> The value of x for the turning point is in the middle of the two roots.

> Substitute the value of x into the equation.

Transformation of the Graph $y = f(x)$

- Functions can be used to describe transformations.

Function	Transformation	
$f(x) + a$	Translation $\binom{0}{a}$	Move up by a
$f(x) - a$	Translation $\binom{0}{-a}$	Move down by a
$f(x + a)$	Translation $\binom{-a}{0}$	Move left by a
$f(x - a)$	Translation $\binom{a}{0}$	Move right by a
$-f(x)$	Reflection in x-axis	
$f(-x)$	Reflection in y-axis	

The curve $y = f(x)$ has a minimum point (2, −3).

Write down the coordinates of the turning point on the curve with equation:

a) $y = f(x + 2)$ — The graph moves left by 2, so the minimum point is (0, −3).

b) $y = f(x) - 3$ — The graph moves down by 3, so the minimum point is (2, −6).

c) $y = -f(x)$ — The graph is reflected in the x-axis, so the maximum point is (2, 3).

> ### Key Point
>
> If the coefficient of the x^2 term is **positive**, the graph will have a **minimum** point. If the coefficient of the x^2 term is **negative**, the graph will have a **maximum** point. The maximum and minimum point can also be found by completing the square (see p.31).

Key Words

quadratic equation
quadratic graph
roots
intercept
turning point
maximum point
minimum point
transformation

Quick Test

1. Sketch the graph of the equation $y = x^2 - 3x + 2$
2. Draw the graph with the equation $y = x^2 - 6$
3. A quadratic function $y = f(x)$ has a maximum at the point (5, 3). Write down the maximum of the curve with equation
   a) $y = f(x) - 1$ and b) $y = f(x - 3)$

Uses of Graphs

You must be able to:

- Use the form $y = mx + c$ to identify parallel and perpendicular lines
- Interpret the gradient of a straight-line graph as a rate of change
- Recognise and interpret graphs that illustrate direct and inverse proportion.

Parallel and Perpendicular Lines

- **Parallel** lines travel in the same direction and have the same gradient.
- **Perpendicular** lines are at right angles to each other.
- If a line has gradient m, then any line perpendicular to it will have a gradient of $-\frac{1}{m}$.

Write down the gradient of the line parallel to the line with the equation $y = 7 - 2x$.

The line has a gradient of -2 so the line that is parallel to it also has a gradient of -2.

 Key Point

The gradient of a straight line in the form $y = mx + c$ is m.

Write down the gradient of the line that is perpendicular to the line with equation $y = 3x - 1$.

The line has a gradient of 3 so the line that is perpendicular to it has a gradient of $-\frac{1}{3}$.

Work out the equation of the line that goes through the point (2, 9) and is parallel to the line with equation $y = 7x + 10$.

$y = mx + c$
$y = 7x + c$ ← Substitute in $m = 7$
$9 = (7 \times 2) + c$ ← Goes through the point (2, 9), so $x = 2$ when $y = 9$
$c = -5$
The equation of the parallel line is $y = 7x - 5$.

Work out the equation of the line that is perpendicular to the line $y = \frac{3}{2}x + 2$ and goes through the point (10, 6).

$y = mx + c$
$y = -\frac{2}{3}x + c$ ← The line has a gradient of $\frac{3}{2}$ so the gradient of the perpendicular line is $-\frac{2}{3}$. This is your value for m.

$6 = (-\frac{2}{3} \times 10) + c$ ← Goes through the point (10, 6), so $x = 10$ when $y = 6$

$c = \frac{38}{3}$

The equation of the perpendicular line is
$y = -\frac{2}{3}x + \frac{38}{3}$ or $3y = 38 - 2x$

Gradient of a Line

- The **rate of change** is the rate at which one quantity changes in relation to another.
- The gradient of a straight-line graph represents a rate of change – it describes how the variable on the y-axis changes when the variable on the x-axis is increased by 1.

The graph below shows the volume of liquid in a container over time. What is the rate of change?

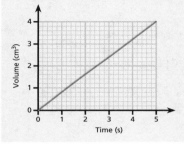

Gradient $= \frac{4}{5}$

$= 0.8 \text{cm}^3/\text{s}$

Gradient $= \dfrac{\text{Change in } y}{\text{Change in } x}$

The gradient is the rate of change.

Real-Life Uses of Graphs

The graph below is the conversion graph between miles and kilometres.

a) How many kilometres are there in 5 miles?

5 miles = 8km

Read from the graph.

b) What is the gradient of the line?

Gradient $= \frac{8}{5}$

$= 1.6$

1 mile = 1.6km

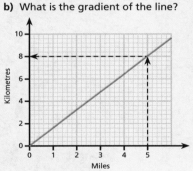

Quick Test

1. Work out the equation of the line that is parallel to the line $y = -2x + 6$ and goes through the point (4, 7).
2. Work out the equation of the line that is perpendicular to the line $y = -2x + 6$ and goes through the point (5, 1).

Key Words

parallel
perpendicular
rate of change

Other Graphs 1

You must be able to:

- Recognise, draw and interpret cubic, reciprocal and exponential graphs
- Interpret distance–time graphs and velocity–time graphs
- Work out acceleration from a velocity–time graph
- Work out speed from a distance–time graph.

Distance–Time Graphs

- A distance–time graph shows distance travelled in relation to a fixed point (starting point) over a period of time.
- The gradient of a straight line joining two points is the speed of travel between those two points.

> **Key Point**
>
>
> $$\text{Speed} = \frac{\text{Distance}}{\text{Time}}$$

The graph below shows Val's car journey from St Bees to Cockermouth and back.

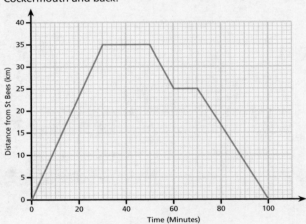

a) Val sets off at 12 noon and travels directly to Cockermouth. At what time does she arrive?

Val travels for 30 minutes so arrives at 12.30pm.

b) For how long does Val stop in Cockermouth?

20 minutes ◄———— *This is represented by the horizontal line on the graph – where the distance does not change.*

c) Val begins her journey home but stops to fill up with petrol. Calculate the average speed of Val's journey from the petrol station to home in kilometres per hour.

$$\text{Speed} = \frac{\text{Distance}}{\text{Time}} = \frac{25}{0.5}$$ ◄———— *Convert minutes into hours.*

$$= 50\text{km/h}$$

Velocity–Time Graphs

- **Velocity** has both magnitude (size) and direction.
- The magnitude of velocity is called speed.
- The gradient of a straight line joining two points is the acceleration between those two points.
- Area Under Graph = Distance Travelled

The graph below shows part of the journey of a car.

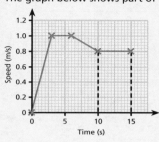

a) For how many seconds does the car decelerate?

4 seconds

b) What is the distance travelled in the last 5 seconds of the journey?

5 × 0.8 = 4m

c) What is the acceleration of the car in the first 3 seconds of the journey?

The acceleration is $\frac{1}{3}$ m/s²

Key Point

A positive gradient shows increasing speed. A negative gradient shows decreasing speed. Zero gradient shows constant speed.

Between 6 seconds and 10 seconds there is a negative gradient, so the car is decelerating.

This is the area of the rectangle under that part of the line.

This is the gradient of the line.

Other Graphs

- A **cubic function** is one that contains an x^3 term.
- A **reciprocal** function takes the form $y = \frac{a}{x}$
- An **exponential** function takes the form $y = k^x$

Cubic Function

Reciprocal Function

Exponential Function

Quick Test

1. Plot the graph $y = 4^x$ for x values –4 to 4.
2. Plot the graph $y = 3x^3 - 5$ for values –2 to 2.
3. Below is a graph for the journey of a car.

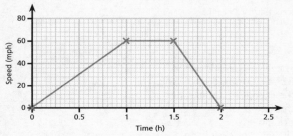

a) What is the total distance travelled?
b) For how many minutes is the car decelerating?

Key Words

distance–time graph
velocity
cubic function
reciprocal
exponential

Other Graphs 2

You must be able to:

- Estimate and interpret the area under a curve
- Work out and interpret a gradient at a point on a curve
- Work out the equation of a tangent to a circle.

Estimating the Area Under a Curve

- On a velocity–time graph, the area under the curve is equal to the distance travelled.
- To estimate the area under a curve, split the area into triangles and trapeziums. Remember, this is only an estimate.

Below is the velocity–time graph for a journey.

Estimate the distance travelled.

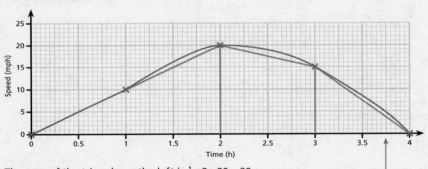

The area of the triangle on the left is $\frac{1}{2} \times 2 \times 20 = 20$

The area of the trapezium is $\frac{1}{2} \times (20 + 15) \times 1 = 17.5$

Look carefully to check the units on the axes match, i.e. time in hours and speed in distance per hour.

The area of the triangle on the right is $\frac{1}{2} \times 1 \times 15 = 7.5$

The total area is $20 + 17.5 + 7.5 = 45$

An estimate of the total distance travelled is 45 miles.

Rates of Change

- The gradient of a straight line describes how the variable on the y-axis changes when the variable on the x-axis is increased by 1 unit.
- On a distance–time graph, speed is the change in distance per unit of time. This is called a rate of change.
- The gradient of a curve is constantly changing.
- The gradient at any particular point is found by drawing a tangent at that point.

Work out the gradient of the curve $y = x^2$ at the point where $x = 3$.

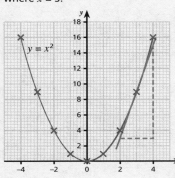

The gradient of the tangent is $\frac{12}{2} = 6$, so the gradient of the curve at $x = 3$ is 6.

Draw a tangent that meets the curve at the specified point.

Equation of a Circle

- The equation of a circle is of the form $x^2 + y^2 = r^2$ where the centre is (0, 0) and the radius is r.
- A circle with equation $x^2 + y^2 = 25$ has centre (0, 0) and radius 5.

Work out the equation of the tangent to the circle with equation $x^2 + y^2 = 25$ at the point (3, 4).

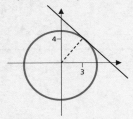

The gradient of the radius is $\frac{4}{3}$.

The gradient (m) of the perpendicular line, i.e. the tangent, is $-\frac{3}{4}$.

$4 = (-\frac{3}{4} \times 3) + c$

$c = \frac{25}{4}$

Substitute $x = 3$, $y = 4$ and $m = -\frac{3}{4}$ into $y = mx + c$ to work out c.

The equation of the tangent is $y = -\frac{3}{4}x + \frac{25}{4}$ OR $4y + 3x = 25$

1. Work out the equation of the tangent of the circle with equation $x^2 + y^2 = 29$ at the point (2, 5).
2. Plot the curve with equation $y = 3x^2 + 5$ and estimate the gradient at the point (2, 17).

Inequalities

You must be able to:

- Solve linear inequalities in one or two variables
- Solve quadratic inequalities in one variable
- Represent solutions to inequalities on number lines or graphs.

Linear Inequalities

- The solution to an **inequality** can be shown on a number line.

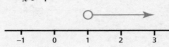

    means $x <$ means $x >$

    means $x \leqslant$ means $x \geqslant$

Solve these inequalities and show the solutions on a number line:

a) $x + 3 > 4$

$x > 4 - 3$

$x > 1$

b) $2(x + 4) \leqslant 18$

$x + 4 \leqslant 9$

$x \leqslant 5$

Work out all the possible integer values of n for these inequalities:

a) $-4 < n < 4$

$n = -3, -2, -1, 0, 1, 2, 3$

b) $-3 < 10n \leqslant 53$

$-0.3 < n \leqslant 5.3$ ← Divide each part of the inequality by 10.

$n = 0, 1, 2, 3, 4, 5$ ← n must be a whole number.

Graphical Inequalities

- The graph of the equation $y = 6$ is a line; the graph of the inequality $y > 6$ is a **region**, which has the line $y = 6$ as a boundary.
- For inequalities $>$ and $<$ the boundary line is **not included** in the solution and is shown as a **dashed line**.
- For inequalities $\geqslant$ and $\leqslant$ the boundary line is **included** in the solution and is shown as a **solid line**.

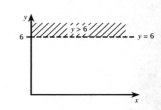

On a graph, show the region that satisfies $x \geq 0$, $x + y < 3$ and $y > 3x - 1$.

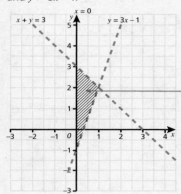

This is the region that satisfies all three inequalities.

Quadratic Inequalities

- A quadratic inequality contains an x^2 term and has a maximum of two possible solutions for x.
- To solve a quadratic inequality you must factorise the side with the quadratic.
- To determine the direction of the arrow for each solution, substitute values for x in the pairs of brackets.

Solve $x^2 + 2x - 15 \geq 0$ and show the solution on a number line.

$(x + 5)(x - 3) \geq 0$ ← Factorise the expression.

If $(x + 5)(x - 3) = 0$, then $x = -5$ or 3

$(x + 5)(x - 3) \geq 0$ ← Substitute values for x to determine the direction of the arrow.

If $x = -10$ then $(-10 + 5)(-10 - 3) = 65$, which satisfies ≥ 0, so the arrow goes to the left from -5.

If $x = 10$, then $(10 + 5)(10 - 3) = 105$, which satisfies ≥ 0, so the arrow goes to the right from 3.

So the solutions are $x \geq 3$ and $x \leq -5$.

Quick Test

1. Solve the inequality $2x - 5 < 9$ and show the solution on a number line.
2. Solve the inequality $5x + 4 < 3x + 10$
3. Solve $x^2 + 5x - 14 \geq 0$

Key Words

inequality
region

Handwritten notes:

$47'19$

cf C.G.P. Rvlep 34

① If $x^2 > a^2$ then $x > a$ or $x \leq a$

② If $x^2 < a^2$ then $-a < x < a$

Review Questions

Basic Algebra & Factorisation and Formulae

1 There are k children in a room.
The number of children who wear glasses is g.

Write an expression in terms of k and g for the number of children who **do not** wear glasses. [1]

2 Simplify $7x - 2y + 5x - 3y$ [2]

3 Work out the value of the following expression when $a = -3$. [1]
$$\frac{4a^2 - a^3}{a^4}$$

4 Expand and simplify $(y + 3)(2y - 7)(6 - y)$ [3]

5 Factorise $5ab - 3b^2c$ [1]

6 Explain why $5p - 7q$ cannot be factorised. [1]

7 Solve $\frac{x}{3} + 3 = 1$ [1]

8 The shape below is a rectangle.

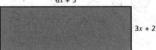

6x + 5

3x + 2

Mitan thinks the correct expression for the perimeter of the rectangle is $9x + 7$.

a) Mitan is wrong. Explain his mistake. [1]

b) The perimeter of the rectangle is 56cm. Work out the value of x. [2]

9 The formula for the volume of a cylinder is $V = \pi r^2 h$.

a) Work out the volume of a cylinder with a radius (r) of 2cm and a height (h) of 10cm. [1]

b) Make r the subject of the formula. [2]

c) Work out the value of r when $V = 50$ and $h = 10$. [2]

Total Marks _____ / 18

Number Patterns and Sequences & Terms and Rules

1 The first term that the following two sequences have in common is 17.

8, 11, 14, 17, 20 …

1, 5, 9, 13, 17 …

Work out the next term that the two sequences have in common.
You must show your working. [2]

2 Regular pentagons of side length 1cm are joined together to make a pattern.

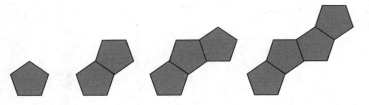

a) Use the patterns to complete the table below.

Pattern Number	Perimeter (cm)
1	
2	
3	
4	
60	
n	

[2]

b) What is the maximum number of pentagons that could be used to give a perimeter less than 1500cm? [2]

3 The nth term of a sequence is $n^2 + 6$.
Jenny states that 'the nth term is odd if n is odd and the nth term is even if n is even'.

Is Jenny correct? Explain your answer. [2]

4 Write down the nth term for the sequence below:

4, 6, 10, 18, 34 … [1]

Total Marks .... / 9

Linear Graphs & Graphs of Quadratic Functions

1   Draw the graph of $y = 4x - 2$ with values of x from -4 to 4.   [2]

2   Draw the graph of the function with gradient 5 and y-intercept $(0, 3)$.   [2]

3   Write down the gradient and y-intercept of the graph with equation $y = 5 - 2x$.   [1]

4   Draw the graph with equation $y = 3x^2 - 2x + 1$ for values of x from -3 to 3.   [2]

5   Work out the equation of the line that joins the points $(-2, 5)$ and $(3, -1)$.   [3]

6   Work out the equation of the line drawn.   [3]

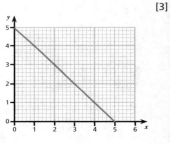

7   A straight line goes through the points (T, S) and (H, R).
$S = R - 5$ and $T = H + 2$

   a) What is the gradient of the line?   [2]

   b) What is the y-intercept in terms of H and R?   [1]

8   The graph has a minimum value at the point $(0, -8)$ and a maximum value at the point $(-2, -4)$.

   Work out the new minimum and maximum values after the following transformations.

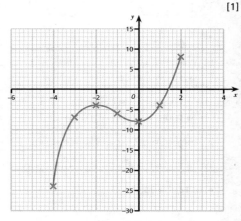

   a) $f(x + 2)$ [2]

   b) $f(-x)$ [2]

   c) $f(x) + 4$ [2]

   d) $f(x - 5)$ [2]

Total Marks _____ / 24

Uses of Graphs & Other Graphs 1 & 2

1   A line is parallel to the line of equation $y = 3x - 2$ and goes through the point (1, 5).

Work out the equation of the line.   [3]

2   Complete the table below.

Gradient of Line	Gradient of Parallel Line	Gradient of Perpendicular Line
5		
	3	
		$-\frac{1}{4}$
$\frac{8}{9}$		

[3]

3   a) On the same set of axes, sketch the graphs of $y = 3^x$ and $y = 5^x$.   [2]

b) Write down one property that the two graphs have in common.   [1]

4   The circle has equation $x^2 + y^2 = 41$

a) Work out the equation of the tangent to the circle at the
point (4, –5).   [4]

b) Write down the equation of a line parallel to the tangent.   [1]

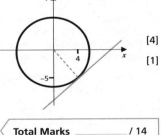

Total Marks _____ / 14

Inequalities

1   Solve $5 - 4x > 25$ and show the answer on a number line.   [2]

2   A bus can carry no more than 52 passengers.

Write down an inequality equation to show this information, where p is the
number of passengers.   [2]

Total Marks _____ / 4

Solving Quadratic Equations

You must be able to:

- Solve quadratic equations by factorising
- Solve quadratic equations by using a graph
- Solve quadratic equations by using the quadratic formula
- Solve quadratic equations by completing the square.

Factorisation

- When solving a quadratic equation by factorisation (see p.5–7), make sure it equals zero first.

> **Key Point**
>
> If two brackets have a product of zero, one of the brackets must equal 0.

Solve the equation $x^2 + 4x + 3 = 0$ by factorisation.

×	x	+1
x	x^2	$+x$
+3	$+3x$	$+3$

Set up and complete a table. The missing terms need to have a product of +3 and a sum of +4.

$(x + 1)(x + 3) = 0$

First row = first bracket; first column = second bracket.

$x + 1 = 0 \qquad x + 3 = 0$

$x = -1 \qquad x = -3$

The Method of Intersection

- Plotting a graph of a quadratic equation can give zero, one or two solutions for x when $y = 0$.
- The solutions are given by the curve's points of intersection with the x-axis. These solutions will sometimes be estimates.

> **Key Point**
>
> The points of intersection with the x-axis are called roots.

Find approximate solutions to the equation $x^2 - 5x + 1 = 0$ by plotting a graph.

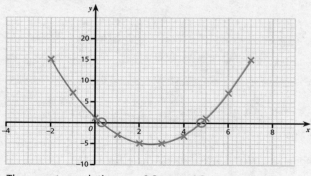

Draw the graph of $y = x^2 - 5x + 1$ (see p.16).

There are two solutions: $x = 0.2$ or $x = 4.8$

These solutions are approximate.

- This method can also be used to solve equations where the solutions are the points of intersection between a curve and a line.

Using the Quadratic Formula

- The quadratic formula is used to solve equations in the form $ax^2 + bx + c = 0$

The quadratic formula is $x = \dfrac{-b \pm \sqrt{b^2 - 4ac}}{2a}$

> **Key Point**
>
> Remember, when calculating b^2, a negative number squared is positive.

Using the quadratic formula, solve $4x^2 - x - 2 = 0$

$$x = \frac{1 \pm \sqrt{(-1)^2 - 4 \times 4 \times (-2)}}{2 \times 4}$$

$x = 0.843$ or -0.593

Substitute in: $a = 4$, $b = -1$, $c = -2$

Completing the Square

- To complete the square, you must write the equation in the form $(x + p)^2 + q = 0$ and then solve it.
- If the coefficient of the x^2 term is not 1, you must take the coefficient out as a factor and then complete the square.

Solve the equation $x^2 - 2x - 2 = 0$

$x^2 - 2x = 2$

$(x - 1)^2 - 1^2 = 2$

$(x - 1)^2 - 1 = 2$

$(x - 1)^2 = 3$

$x = 1 \pm \sqrt{3}$

Move the constant over to the right-hand side.

The number in the brackets is always half the coefficient of x.

Always minus the square of that number.

Solve.

[handwritten annotations:] $(x-1)(x-1)$ $x^2 - 2x + 1 - 3 = 0$ $(x=1)^2 = 3$ $x - 1 = \sqrt{3}$ $x = 1 + \sqrt{3}$

Iteration

- Iteration is the repetition of a mathematical procedure.
- The results of one iteration are used as the starting point for the next.

> **Key Point**
>
> Iteration involves solving an equation many times. With each iteration your answer becomes more accurate.

Solve $x^2 - 3x - 1 = 0$ using iteration, to 2 decimal places.

$x = \dfrac{1}{x - 3}$ or $x = \dfrac{1}{x} + 3$

$x_{n+1} = \dfrac{1}{x_n - 3}$ or $x_{n+1} = \dfrac{1}{x_n} + 3$

The solutions are $x = -0.30$ and $x = 3.30$

Rearrange to make x the subject.

These two equations give the two solutions.

Substitute in any value for x_n. Use the results as a starting point for the next substitution. Continue until the terms converge.

> **Key Words**
>
> factorisation
> intersection
> complete the square
> coefficient
> iteration

Quick Test

1. Solve the equation $x^2 = 2x + 5$ by the method of intersection.
2. Solve the equation $3x^2 - 5x - 1 = 0$ using the quadratic formula.
3. Solve the equation $x^2 - 4x + 2 = 0$ by completing the square.
4. Solve $x^2 - 5x - 1 = 0$ using iteration (to 2 d.p.).

Simultaneous Equations and Functions

You must be able to:

- Solve linear and quadratic simultaneous equations algebraically
- Find approximate solutions to simultaneous equations using a graph
- Translate simple situations into two simultaneous equations and solve
- Work out composite functions.

Algebraic Methods

- Linear simultaneous equations can be solved by elimination.

> Solve the following simultaneous equations:
>
> $3x - y = 18$ Equation 1
> $x + y = 10$ Equation 2
> $4x = 28$ $7 + y = 10$
> $x = 7$ $y = 3$

Key Point

Solutions to simultaneous equations always come in pairs.

Add equation 1 and equation 2 to eliminate the y terms.

Substitute your value for x into one of the equations.

> Annabel buys three pears and two apples for £1.20
> David buys four pears and three apples for £1.65
>
> Work out the cost of one apple and one pear.
>
> $3p + 2a = 120$ Equation 1
> $4p + 3a = 165$ Equation 2
> Equation 1 × 4: $12p + 8a = 480$
> Equation 2 × 3: $12p + 9a = 495$
> $a = 15$
> $3p + (2 \times 15) = 120$
> $p = 30$
> An apple costs 15p and a pear costs 30p.

Form two equations with the information given.

Multiply so that the p terms match. Remember to multiply all terms.

Subtract equation 1 from equation 2.

Substitute your value for a into one of the equations and solve.

- When you have a non-linear equation and a linear equation, always substitute the linear into the non-linear.

> Solve the equations $2y + x = 3x^2$ and $y + 5x = -3$
>
> $2y + x = 3x^2$ Equation 1
> $y + 5x = -3$ Equation 2
> $y = -3 - 5x$
> $2 \times (-3 - 5x) + x = 3x^2$
> $3x^2 + 9x + 6 = 0$
> $x^2 + 3x + 2 = 0$
> $(x + 1)(x + 2) = 0$
> $x = -1, y = 2$ or $x = -2, y = 7$

Make y the subject of equation 2.

Substitute into equation 1.

This is a quadratic equation; rearrange to = 0.

Divide all terms by 3.

Solve by factorisation.

Solving Equations with Graphs

- You can plot graphs and find the point of intersection. However, the solutions will often only be approximate.

Solve the equations $y = 3x^2$ and $y + 5x = 3$

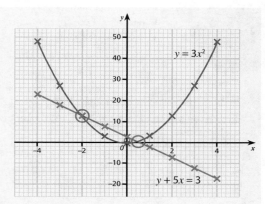

The points of intersection are (–2.1, 13.5) and (0.5, 1).

So, the two approximate solutions are $x = 0.5$, $y = 1$ or $x = –2.1$, $y = 13.5$

Functions

- Functions have an **input** and an **output**, e.g.

  If $f(x) = 4x + 2$ $f(5) = 4 \times 5 + 2 = 22$ ←   5 is the input of the function, so substitute for x.

- The inverse function is the reverse process of the function, e.g.

  If $f(x) = 4x + 2$ $f^{-1}(x) = \dfrac{x - 2}{4}$

> **Key Point**
>
> The inverse function is written as $f^{-1}(x)$.

- A **composite function** is when one function becomes the input of another, e.g.

  $g(x) = 3x - 2$

  $f(x) = 2x^2 + 5$

  a) Work out $fg(x)$ ←
  $\quad fg(x) = f(3x - 2)$
  $\quad\quad = 2(3x - 2)^2 + 5$
  $\quad\quad = 18x^2 - 24x + 13$ ←

  b) Work out $gf(x)$ ←
  $\quad gf(x) = g(2x^2 + 5)$
  $\quad\quad = 3(2x^2 + 5) - 2$
  $\quad\quad = 6x^2 + 13$ ←

This means make $g(x)$ the input of $f(x)$.

Expand the brackets to simplify.

This means make $f(x)$ the input of $g(x)$.

Expand the brackets to simplify.

> **Key Words**
>
> linear equation
> simultaneous equations
> function
> input
> output
> composite functions

Quick Test

1. Solve the simultaneous equations $2x + y = 5$ and $x + y = 3$
2. Solve the simultaneous equations $y = 3x - 1$ and $y = x^2 - 5$
3. Solve the simultaneous equations $y = x$ and $y = x^2 - 2$ using a graph.
4. If $f(x) = 3x + 1$ and $g(x) = 2x^2 + 5$, work out $gf(x)$.

Algebraic Proof

You must be able to:

- Argue mathematically
- Use algebra to support and construct arguments
- Include proofs in your arguments.

Using Algebra

- Algebra can be used to determine if a statement is:
  - always true
  - true for certain values
  - never true.
- An identity is an equation that is true no matter what values are chosen.

> *The sum of any three consecutive integers is always a multiple of 3.*
>
> Is this statement true? You must show your working.
>
> Let n represent the first integer.
> The second integer is $n + 1$ and the third integer is $n + 2$.
> The sum is: $n + (n + 1) + (n + 2) \equiv 3n + 3$
> This can be written as $3(n + 1)$
> Therefore, the sum of three consecutive integers is always a multiple of 3. The statement is **always** true.

> *The sum of the squares of any three consecutive integers is always a multiple of 3.*
>
> Is this statement true? You must show your working.
>
> Let n represent the first integer.
> The second integer is $n + 1$ and the third integer is $n + 2$.
> The sum of the squares is: $n^2 + (n + 1)^2 + (n + 2)^2 \equiv 3n^2 + 6n + 5$
> 3 is **not** a factor of this expression, therefore the statement is **never** true.

Key Point

$\equiv$ means **always** equal to

$\equiv$ is the identity sign and it means that any equation it is used in will always be true for any value of the variable(s).

Algebraic Proof

- Algebra can be used to help construct an argument.
- Proofs are examples of mathematical reasoning, used in an argument, to show a statement is true, i.e. they provide evidence for an argument.

The median of three consecutive integers is n. Show that the mean is also n.

The median is the middle number, so the three consecutive integers in terms of n are: $n - 1$, n, $n + 1$

$$\text{Mean} = \frac{(n - 1) + n + (n + 1)}{3} = \frac{3n}{3} = n$$

Show that $\dfrac{3}{x + 1} + \dfrac{3x}{x^2 + 3x + 2} \equiv \dfrac{6}{x + 2}$

$$\frac{3}{x + 1} + \frac{3x}{x^2 + 3x + 2} \equiv \frac{3}{x + 1} + \frac{3x}{(x + 1)(x + 2)}$$

> Start with the LHS (left-hand side). Factorise the denominator.

$$\frac{3}{x + 1} + \frac{3x}{(x + 1)(x + 2)} \equiv \frac{3(x + 2)}{(x + 1)(x + 2)} + \frac{3x}{(x + 1)(x + 2)}$$

> Find a common denominator.

$$\frac{3(x + 2)}{(x + 1)(x + 2)} + \frac{3x}{(x + 1)(x + 2)} \equiv \frac{3(x + 2) + 3x}{(x + 1)(x + 2)}$$

> Simplify.

$$\frac{3(x + 2) + 3x}{(x + 1)(x + 2)} \equiv \frac{6x + 6}{(x + 1)(x + 2)}$$

$$\frac{6x + 6}{(x + 1)(x + 2)} \equiv \frac{6(x + 1)}{(x + 1)(x + 2)}$$

> Factorise the numerator.

$$\frac{6(x + 1)}{(x + 1)(x + 2)} \equiv \frac{6}{(x + 2)} = \text{RHS}$$

> Cancel down.

The diagram shows two squares. The blue square has a side length of $2n$.

Show that the ratio of the area of the green square to the area of the blue square is 1 : 2

Key Point

Always show every stage of your working.

Area of blue square is: $2n \times 2n = 4n^2$

The side length of the green square is: $\sqrt{n^2 + n^2} = \sqrt{2n^2}$

> Use Pythagoras' Theorem.

The area of the green square is: $\sqrt{2n^2} \times \sqrt{2n^2} = 2n^2$

Ratio of areas is: $2n^2 : 4n^2$, which simplifies to 1 : 2

Quick Test

1. Show that the sum of any two consecutive integers will always be an odd number.
2. Show that the difference of the squares of two consecutive integers will always be an odd number.
3. A set of five consecutive integers has a median of n. Work out the mean in terms of n.
4. Show that $\dfrac{2}{x} + \dfrac{3}{x^2} \equiv \dfrac{2x + 3}{x^2}$

Key Words

identity
argument
proof

Linear Graphs & Graphs of Quadratic Functions

1. Work out the equation of the line that joins the points $\left(\frac{2}{3}, 8\right)$ and $\left(\frac{5}{6}, 5\right)$. [3]

2. Work out the equation of the line drawn below. [3]

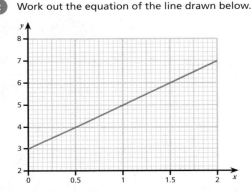

3. Sketch the graph of the function $y = x^2 + 4x + 3$, clearly stating the roots and the coordinates of the turning point. [3]

4. The equation of a line is $4y = 3x + 1$

   Work out the gradient and y-intercept of the line. [2]

5. A curve has the equation $y = x^2 + ax + b$
   The curve crosses the x-axis at the points $(-7, 0)$ and $(1, 0)$.

   a) Work out the values of a and b. [3]

   b) Work out the coordinates of the turning point. [2]

6. a) Sketch the graph $y = \frac{1}{x}$ [1]

   b) On the same axes sketch the graph $y = -\frac{1}{x}$ [1]

   c) Describe two different transformations that will transform the graph in part a) to the graph in part b). [2]

   Total Marks _____ / 20

Uses of Graphs & Other Graphs 1 & 2

1 Line 1 has equation $5y = 3x - 2$
Line 2 has equation $3y + 5x = 6$

Show that line 1 and line 2 are perpendicular. [2]

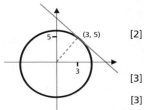

2 A circle has centre (0, 0) and goes through the point (3, 5).

a) Work out the equation of the circle. [3]

b) Work out the equation of the tangent to the circle at the point (3, 5). [3]

3 **a)** Expand $(x - 3)(x + 3)(x - 2)$ [3]

b) Sketch the graph of $(x - 3)(x + 3)$ [2]

4 Work out the equation of the line that is perpendicular to the line with equation
$2y + x = 5$ and goes through the point (3, 6). [3]

Total Marks _____ / 16

Inequalities

1 Work out all the possible integer values for y if $12 \leqslant 3y \leqslant 36$. [2]

2 Solve $x^2 + 5x - 24 \geqslant 0$ [3]

3 Solve $2 - 9x > 3$ and show the solution on a number line. [2]

4 A TV salesperson is set a target to sell more than six televisions a week.
The manufacturer can let the salesperson have a maximum of 20 televisions each week.

Use an inequality equation to represent the number of televisions that could be sold
each week if the salesperson meets or exceeds their target. [2]

Total Marks _____ / 9

Practice Questions

Solving Quadratic Equations

1 Solve the equation $3x^2 = 27$ [1]

2 **a)** Write $x^2 + 8x - 12$ in the form $(x + p)^2 + q$, where p and q are integers. [2]

b) Solve the equation $x^2 + 8x - 12 = 0$ giving your answer in the form $a \pm b\sqrt{7}$. [2]

c) Write down the minimum point of $y = x^2 + 8x - 12$ [1]

3 The diagram shows a trapezium. All the measurements are in centimetres. The area of the trapezium is 14cm².

a) Show that $6x^2 - 5x - 14 = 0$ [3]

b) Solve the equation to find the value of x. [2]

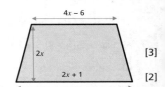

Total Marks _____ / 11

Simultaneous Equations and Functions

1 **a)** On the same set of axes, draw the graphs $y = 2x^2$ and $y = 3x + 2$ [2]

b) Use your graph to solve the equation $2x^2 = 3x + 2$ [2]

2 Solve the simultaneous equations: [4]

$$2x + y = 1$$
$$y = x^2 - 2$$

3 $f(x) = x^2 + 1$ and $g(x) = 3x - 2$

a) Work out $fg(x)$ [2]

b) $fg(x) = gf(x)$

Show that this statement is incorrect. [2]

c) Use the quadratic formula to solve the equation $fg(x) = 10$ [3]

Total Marks _____ / 15

Algebraic Proof

1 Prove that the sum of the squares of any three consecutive integers is 1 less than a multiple of 3. [3]

2 Grace surprises her friends with the following number trick:
- Think of a number.
- Multiply your number by 3.
- Add 30 to your answer.
- Divide your number by 3.
- Subtract the number you first thought of.
- Your answer is 10.

Use algebra to prove that Grace's trick always works. [3]

3 Show that $\dfrac{3}{x+2} + \dfrac{9}{x^2+x-2} = \dfrac{3}{x-1}$ [3]

4 Show that $\dfrac{6}{3x+2} + \dfrac{4}{3x-2} \equiv \dfrac{30x-4}{9x^2-4}$ [3]

5 The diagram below shows a circle inside a square. The square has a side length of $6x$.

Show that the ratio of the area of the square to the area of the circle is $4 : \pi$ [4]

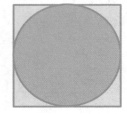

6 Prove that $(4n+1)^2 - (4n-1)^2$ is a multiple of 8 for all positive integer values of n. [3]

7 Prove that the difference between the squares of any two consecutive even numbers is always a multiple of 4. [3]

8 a and b are numbers such that $a = b + 2$

The sum of a and b is equal to the product of a and b.

Show that a and b are **not** integers. [3]

Total Marks _____ / 25

Review Questions

Solving Quadratic Equations

1 A circle has equation $x^2 + y^2 = 36$

   a) Write down the equation of the tangent shown
       on the diagram.   [1]

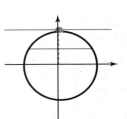

   b) A chord, as shown on the diagram, goes through
       the point (0, 3) and intersects the circle in two places.
       Work out the points of intersection.   [3]

2 **a)** Write $x^2 - 12x + 26$ in the form $(x + p)^2 + q$.   [3]

   b) Use your answer from part **a)** to solve the equation $x^2 - 12x + 26 = 0$
       Leave your answers in surd form.   [2]

3 Solve the equation $\dfrac{4}{x} + \dfrac{4}{x + 2} = 3$ [4]

4 The area of the triangle is 4cm^2.

   Work out the value of x. Give your answer in the form $a\sqrt{6}$.   [3]

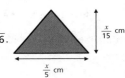

5 Use the quadratic formula to solve the equation $x^2 - 7x - 15 = 0$ [2]

                                                Total Marks _____ / 18

Simultaneous Equations and Functions

1 **a)** On the same axes, draw the graphs of $y = 3x^2$ and $y = 4x + 2$.   [2]

   b) Use your graphs to find estimates to the solutions of the equation $3x^2 = 4x + 2$ [2]

2 Solve the following simultaneous equations:

   $y - x = 4$

   $y = x^2 + 2$ [4]

                                                Total Marks _____ / 8

Algebraic Proof

1 **a)** Write down the expression for the nth term of the sequence 4, 7, 10, 13, 16 ... [1]

    b) Prove that the product of any two consecutive terms in this sequence is also a term
       of the sequence. [3]

2 Prove algebraically that the difference between the squares of any two consecutive
integers is equal to the sum of these two integers. [3]

3 Show that $\dfrac{x^2 + 5x + 6}{x^2 + 2x} = \dfrac{x + 3}{x}$ [3]

4 Jessa thinks that when you subtract 7 from a number, the answer is always odd.

    Give an example to show that Jessa is wrong. [1]

5 The shape shown is a square.

    Emma states that the area of the square is half of the product of the diagonals.
    Prove that Emma is correct. [2]

6 Prove that $(3n + 1)^2 - (3n - 1)^2$ is a multiple of 4 for all positive integer values of n. [3]

7 Here is a sequence of numbers:
    2, 5, 10, 17, 26, 37 ...

    a) Write down the expression for the nth term of this sequence. [1]

    b) Show algebraically that the sum of two consecutive terms in this sequence
       will always be odd. [3]

8 Show that $\dfrac{2}{x - 2} - \dfrac{8}{x^2 - 4} \equiv \dfrac{2}{x + 2}$ [3]

9 Prove that the square of any odd number is always one more than a multiple of 4. [3]

10 *'The sum of two prime numbers is also a prime number.'*

    Give an example to disprove this statement. [1]

Total Marks _____ / 27

Answers

Pages 4–11 Revise Questions

Page 5 Quick Test
1. $6y - 5$
2. -171
3. $12t^2 - 3t$
4. $2r^2(2r - 1)$
5. $t = -0.25$ OR $-\frac{1}{4}$

Page 7 Quick Test
1. $w = 9$
2. $y^2 + 2y - 8$
3. $(2q + 1)(q + 3)$
4. $y = \frac{x + 6}{5}$

Page 9 Quick Test
1. $-4, -8$
2. $-2, 43$
3. 72

Page 11 Quick Test
1. a) $3n + 4$
   b) 154
2. $31, 44$
3. $n^3 - 1$

Pages 12–13 Practice Questions

Page 12
1. $9x + 4y$ **[2]**
2. $4y - 8z + 12$ **[2]**
3. $4x^2 + 2x + 4$ **[2]**
4. 23 **[1]**
5. $8b = 14$ OR $2b = \frac{7}{2}$ **[1]**; $b = \frac{7}{4}$ OR $1\frac{3}{4}$ **[1]**
6. $3p + 6 = 2p + 6$ **[1]**; $p = 0$ **[1]**
7. $\frac{5}{2}x - \frac{2}{3}x = \frac{1}{2} + \frac{1}{3}$ **[1]**; $\frac{15}{6}x - \frac{4}{6}x = \frac{3}{6} + \frac{2}{6}$ **[1]**; $x = \frac{5}{11}$ **[1]**

> Look for a common denominator.

8. $6x - 30y + 36$ **[2]** (1 mark for 2 correct terms)
9. $6p - 4q + 12$ **[2]**

> $- \times - = +$

10. $4xz(y - 1)$ **[2]** OR $4z(yx - x)$ **[1]** OR $4x(yz - z)$ **[1]**
11. $(w^2 + 5w + 4)(w - 4)$ **[1]**; $w^3 + 5w^2 + 4w - 4w^2 - 20w - 16$ **[1]**; $w^3 + w^2 - 16w - 16$ **[1]**
12. $(x + 1)(x + 2)$ **[2]**
13. $6x - 15 + 4x + 12 - 4x$ **[1]**; $6x - 3$ **[1]**; $3(2x - 1)$ **[1]**
14. $4xy + 2y = 1 - 3x$ **[1]**; $y(4x + 2) = 1 - 3x$ **[1]**; $y = \frac{1 - 3x}{4x + 2}$ **[1]**
15. a) $2A = (a + b)h$ **[1]**, $h = \frac{2A}{a + b}$ **[1]**
    b) $h = \frac{48}{5 + 7}$ **[1]**; 4cm **[1]**
16. $(x + 3)(x + 2)$ **[2]**
17. a) $V = \sqrt{50}$ **[1]**; $= 5\sqrt{2}$ OR 7.07 **[1]**
    b) $V^2 = u^2 - 10p$ **[1]**; $u = \sqrt{V^2 + 10p}$ **[1]**

Page 13
1. $24 - 4n$ **[2]**
2. $-2, 1, 4, 7, 10$ **[2]** (1 mark for any three correct)
3. a) $3n + 11$ **[2]**
   b) 311 **[1]**
4. a) $P = 10 \times 2^0$ **[1]**; $P = 10$ **[1]**
   b) $P = 10 \times 2^5$ **[1]**; $P = 320$ **[1]**
   c) $2^t = 100$ **[1]**; $t = 7$ hours **[1]**
   d) No, as the population will have a limit. **[1]**
5. a) $30, 48$ **[2]**
   b) 3 **[1]**
6. a)
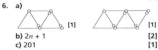
[1] **[1]**
   b) $2n + 1$ **[2]**
   c) 201 **[1]**
7.

n	0	1	2	3	4	5
c	-1	4	15	32	55	84
$a + b$	5	11	17	23	29	
$2a$	6	6	6	6		

A complete table or equivalent working **[1]**; $a = 3$, $b = 2$, $c = -1$ **[1]**; $3n^2 + 2n - 1$ **[1]**

Pages 14–25 Revise Questions

Page 15 Quick Test
1.
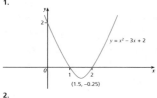
2. Gradient $= -2$ and y-intercept $= (0,5)$
3. $y = -1.5x + 14.5$ OR $2y + 3x - 29 = 0$

Page 17 Quick Test
1.
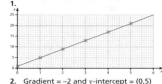
2.
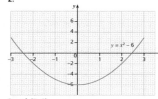
3. a) $(5, 2)$
   b) $(8, 3)$

Page 19 Quick Test
1. $y = -2x + 15$
2. $y = 0.5x - 1.5$ OR $2y = x - 3$

Page 21 Quick Test
1.
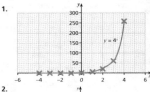
2.
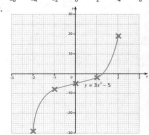
3. a) 75 miles
   b) 30 minutes

Page 23 Quick Test
1. $y = -\frac{2}{5}x + \frac{29}{5}$ OR $5y = 29 - 2x$
2. 12 (approximately)

Page 25 Quick Test
1.
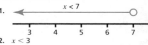
$x < 7$
2. $x < 3$
3. Solutions are $x \geqslant 2$ and $x \leqslant -7$

Pages 26–27 Review Questions

Page 26
1. $k - g$ **[1]**
2. $12x - 5y$ **[2]**
3. $\frac{7}{9}$ OR 0.7 **[1]**
4. $(2y^2 - y - 21)(6 - y)$ **[1]**; $12y^2 - 6y - 126 - 2y^3 + y^2 + 21y$ **[1]**; $-2y^3 + 13y^2 + 15y - 126$ **[1]**
5. $b(5a - 3bc)$ **[1]**
6. 5 and 7 are prime numbers, so there are no common factors. **[1]**
7. $x = -6$ **[1]**
8. a) He has only found half of the perimeter. **[1]**
   b) $18x + 14 = 56$ **[1]**; $x = \frac{7}{3} = 2\frac{1}{3}$ cm **[1]**
9. a) $\pi \times 2^2 \times 10 = 125.66\text{cm}^3$ **[1]**
   b) $r^2 = \frac{V}{\pi h}$ **[1]**; $r = \sqrt{\frac{V}{\pi h}}$ **[1]**
   c) $r = \sqrt{\frac{50}{\pi \times 10}}$ **[1]**; $r = 1.26$ (to 3 significant figures) **[1]**

Page 27
1. LCM of 3 and 4 = 12 **[1]**; therefore, 29 will be common to both **[1]**
2. a)

Pattern Number	Perimeter (cm)
1	5
2	8
3	11
4	14
60	182 **[1]**
n	$3n + 2$ **[1]**

b) $3n + 2 < 1500$ **[1]**; 499 pentagons **[1]**
3. Yes, Jenny is correct. For n^2, even multiplied by even is even and odd multiplied by odd is odd. **[1]**; For $n^2 + 6$, even + 6 = even and odd + 6 = odd **[1]**
4. $2^n + 2$ **[1]**

Page 28
1. Fully correct graph with y-intercept at (0, −2) **[1]**; and a straight line crossing through points (−4, −18) and (4, 14) **[1]**

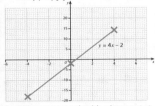

2. Fully correct graph with y-intercept at (0, 3) **[1]**; and a straight line crossing through points (−2,−7) and (2,13) **[1]**

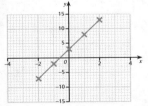

3. Gradient = −2 and y-intercept = (0, 5) **[1]**

4. Fully correct table **[1]**; and accurately plotted graph **[1]**

x	−3	−2	−1	0	1	2	3
y	34	17	6	1	2	9	22

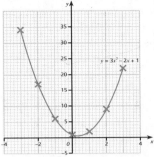

$y = 3x^2 - 2x + 1$

5. $m = \dfrac{-1-5}{3-(-2)} = \dfrac{-6}{5}$ **[1]**;

$5 = \dfrac{-6}{5} \times \dfrac{-2}{1} + c, c = \dfrac{13}{5}$ **[1]**;

$y = \dfrac{-6}{5}x + \dfrac{13}{5}$ OR $5y = -6x + 13$ **[1]**
6. $m = -1$ **[1]**; $c = 5$ **[1]**; $y = 5 - x$ OR $x + y = 5$ **[1]**
7. a) $m = \dfrac{R - (R - 5)}{H - (H + 2)}$ **[1]** $= \dfrac{5}{-2}$ **[1]**

b) $c = R + \dfrac{5}{2}H$ **[1]**
8. a) Minimum (−2, −8) **[1]**; maximum (−4, −4) **[1]**
b) Minimum (0, −8) **[1]**; maximum (2, −4) **[1]**
c) Minimum (0, −4) **[1]**; maximum (−2, 0) **[1]**
d) Minimum (5, −8) **[1]**; maximum (3, −4) **[1]**

Page 29
1. $m = 3$ **[1]**; $5 = 3 + c, c = 2$ **[1]**; $y = 3x + 2$ **[1]**
2. Table correctly complete (deduct 1 mark for one error and 2 marks for two errors; 0 marks for more than two errors) **[3]**

Gradient of Line	Gradient of Parallel Line	Gradient of Perpendicular Line
5	5	$-\dfrac{1}{5}$
3	3	$-\dfrac{1}{3}$
4	4	$-\dfrac{1}{4}$
$\dfrac{8}{9}$	$\dfrac{8}{9}$	$-\dfrac{9}{8}$

3. a) Sketch showing the two curved lines **[1]** intersecting the y-axis at (0, 1) **[1]**

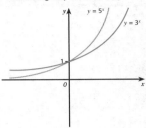

$y = 5^x$
$y = 3^x$

b) Both pass through point (0, 1) **[1]**
4. a) Gradient of radius = $-\dfrac{5}{4}$ **[1]**;

Gradient of tangent = $\dfrac{4}{5}$ **[1]**;

$-5 = \dfrac{4}{5} \times 4 + c, c = -\dfrac{41}{5}$ **[1]**;

$y = \dfrac{4}{5}x - \dfrac{41}{5}$ OR $5y = 4x - 41$ **[1]**

b) $y = \dfrac{4}{5}x +$ any value **[1]**

1. $-4x > 20$ **[1]**; $x < -5$

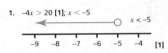

$x < -5$

$-9 \quad -8 \quad -7 \quad -6 \quad -5 \quad -4$ **[1]**

If x is negative the inequality sign will change direction.

2. $0 < p < 52$ where p is the number of passengers **[2]**

Page 31 Quick Test
1. $x = -1.4$ or 3.4
2. $x = 1.85$ or −0.18
3. $x = 2 \pm \sqrt{2}$
4. $x = 5.19$ or −0.19

Page 33 Quick Test
1. $x = 2, y = 1$
2. $x = 4, y = 11$ and $x = -1, y = -4$
3. $x = 2, y = 2$ and $x = -1, y = -1$
4. $18x^2 + 12x + 7$

Page 35 Quick Test
1. $n + (n + 1) = 2n + 1$, $2n$ is even, therefore $2n + 1$ is odd.
2. n^2 and $(n + 1)^2$, n^2 and $n^2 + 2n + 1$. The difference is $2n + 1$, which is an odd number.
3. Set of integers is $n - 2, n - 1, n, n + 1, n + 2$. Mean $= \dfrac{5n}{5} = n$
4. $\dfrac{2}{x} + \dfrac{3}{x^2} = \dfrac{2x}{x^2} + \dfrac{3}{x^2} = \dfrac{2x + 3}{x^2}$

Answers

Page 36

1. $m = \dfrac{5-8}{\frac{2}{3}-\frac{2}{3}} = -18$ [1];

$8 = -18 \times \left(\dfrac{2}{3}\right) + c, c = 20$ [1];

$y = -18x + 20$ [1]

2. $m = \dfrac{4}{2} = 2$ [1];

y-intercept $= (0, 3)$[1];

$y = 2x + 3$ [1]

3. $(x + 1)(x + 3)$[1]; $x = -1$ and $x = -3$ [1];

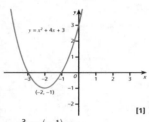

[1]

4. $m = \dfrac{3}{4}$ [1]; $\left(0, \dfrac{1}{4}\right)$[1]

5. a) $y = (x + 7)(x - 1)$ [1]; $x^2 + 6x - 7$ [1]; $a = 6, b = -7$ [1]

b) $y = (x + 3)^2 - 16$[1]; $(-3, -16)$ [1]

6. a)

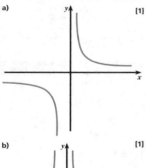

[1]

b)

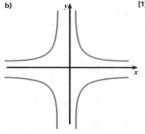

[1]

c) Any two from: Reflection in y-axis; Reflection in x-axis; Rotation 90° clockwise about (0, 0); Rotation 90°

anticlockwise about (0, 0). [2]

Page 37

1. $m_1 = \dfrac{3}{5}, m_2 = -\dfrac{5}{3}$ [1]; $\dfrac{3}{5} \times -\dfrac{5}{3} = -1$ [1]

2. a) $r^2 = 3^2 + 5^2$ [1]; $r^2 = 34$ [1];
$x^2 + y^2 = 34$ [1]

b) Gradient of radius $= \dfrac{5}{3}$ [1]; Gradient of tangent $= -\dfrac{3}{5}$ [1]; $5y + 3x = 34$ or equivalent [1]

3. a) $(x - 3)(x + 3) = x^2 - 9$ [1];
$(x^2 - 9)(x - 2)$ [1]; $x^3 - 2x^2 - 9x + 18$ [1]

b)

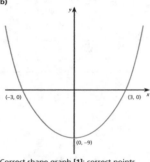

Correct shape graph [1]; correct points of intersection [1]

4. $m_1 = -\dfrac{1}{2}, m_2 = 2$ [1]; $6 = 2 \times 3 + c$,
$c = 0$ [1]; $y = 2x$ [1]

1. $4 \leqslant y \leqslant 12$ [1]; 4, 5, 6, 7, 8, 9, 10, 11, 12 [1]
2. $(x + 8)(x - 3) \geqslant 0$ [1]; one solution is $x \leqslant -8$ [1]; one solution is $x \geqslant 3$ [1]

3. $-9x > 1, x < -\dfrac{1}{9}$ [1]

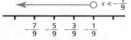

[1]

4. If t is number of televisions, $t > 6$ and $t \leqslant 20$ [1]; $6 < t \leqslant 20$ [1]

Page 38

1. $x = \pm 3$ [1]

2. a) $(x + 4)^2 - 28$, $p = 4$ [1]; $q = -28$ [1]

b) $x = -4 \pm \sqrt{28}$ [1]; $x = -4 \pm 2\sqrt{7}$ [1]

c) $(-4, -28)$ [1]

3. a) $A = \dfrac{1}{2}(a + b)h$,

$14 = \dfrac{1}{2}(4x - 6 + 2x + 1)\,2x$ [1];

$14 = \dfrac{1}{2}(12x^2 - 10x)$ [1];

$6x^2 - 5x - 14 = 0$ [1]

b) $(6x + 7)(x - 2)$ [1]; $x = 2$ [1]

> If x is a length it must be positive.

1. a) Straight-line graph correct [1]; and curved graph correct [1]

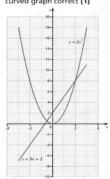

b) $(-0.5, 0.5)$ [1]; $(2, 8)$ [1]

> When graphs of simultaneous equations are plotted, the x-coordinates of the points of intersection give you your solutions.

2. $y = 1 - 2x$ [1]; $1 - 2x = x^2 - 2$ [1];
$x^2 + 2x - 3 = 0$, $(x + 3)(x - 1) = 0$ [1];
$(-3, 7)$, $(1, -1)$ OR $x = -3$, $y = 7$ or $x = 1$, $y = -1$ [1]

3. a) $f(3x - 2) = (3x - 2)^2 + 1$ [1];
$fg(x) = 9x^2 - 12x + 5$ [1]

b) $gf(x) = 3(x^2 + 1) - 2$ [1];
$= 3x^2 + 1 \neq 9x^2 - 12x + 5$ [1]

c) $9x^2 - 12x - 5 = 0$ [1];
$x = \dfrac{12 \pm \sqrt{(-12)^2 - 4 \times 9 \times (-5)}}{18}$ [1];
$x = \dfrac{5}{3}$ or $-\dfrac{1}{3}$ [1]

Page 39

1. $n^2 + (n + 1)^2 + (n + 2)^2$ [1]; $3n^2 + 6n + 5$ [1]; $3(n^2 + 2n + 2) - 1$, which is 1 less than a multiple of 3 [1]

2. Let n = chosen number [1]; [1]
$\dfrac{3n + 30}{3} = n + 10$ [1]; $n + 10 - n = 10$ [1];

3. $\dfrac{3}{x + 2} + \dfrac{9}{(x + 2)(x - 1)}$ [1]; $\dfrac{3(x - 1) + 9}{(x + 2)(x - 1)}$ [1];
$\dfrac{3x - 3 + 9}{(x + 2)(x - 1)} = \dfrac{3(x + 2)}{(x + 2)(x - 1)} = \dfrac{3}{(x - 1)}$ [1]

4. $\dfrac{6(3x - 2)}{(3x + 2)(3x - 2)} + \dfrac{4(3x + 2)}{(3x + 2)(3x - 2)}$ [1];
$\dfrac{18x - 12 + 12x + 8}{9x^2 - 4}$ [1]; $\dfrac{30x - 4}{9x^2 - 4}$ [1]

> Find a common denominator.

5. Area of square $= 36x^2$ [1];
Area of circle $= \pi(3x)^2 = 9\pi x^2$ [1];

$36x^2 : 9\pi x^2$ **[1]**; $4 : \pi$ **[1]**

6. $(16n^2 + 8n + 1) - (16n^2 - 8n + 1)$ **[1]**;
$16n$ **[1]**; $8(2n)$ which is a multiple of 8 **[1]**

7. $(2n + 2)^2 - (2n)^2$ **[1]**; $8n + 4$ **[1]**; $4(2n + 1)$
which is a multiple of 4 **[1]**

8. $a + b = ab$ **[1]**; $b + 2 + b = b(b + 2)$ **[1]**;
$b^2 = 2$, therefore b is not an integer,
and $a = \sqrt{2} + 2$, so a is not an integer. **[1]**

Pages 40–41 Review Questions

Page 40

1. a) $y = 6$ **[1]**
b) $x^2 + (3)^2 = 36$, $x^2 = 27$ **[1]**;
$x = \pm3\sqrt{3}$ OR $x = 5.2$ or -5.2 **[1]**; Points
of intersection (5.2, 3) and (-5.2, 3) **[1]**

2. a) $(x - 6)^2 - 10$ **[1]**; $p = -6$ **[1]**; $q = -10$ **[1]**;
b) $(x - 6)^2 = 10$, $x - 6 = \pm\sqrt{10}$ **[1]**;
$x = 6 + \sqrt{10}$, $x = 6 - \sqrt{10}$ **[1]**

3. $\dfrac{4(x + 2)}{x(x + 2)} + \dfrac{4x}{x(x + 2)} = 3$ **[1]**; $\dfrac{8x + 8}{x^2 + 2x} = 3$,
$8x + 8 = 3x^2 + 6x$ **[1]**; $3x^2 - 2x - 8 = 0$ **[1]**; $(3x + 4)(x - 2)$,
$x = -\dfrac{4}{3}$ and $x = 2$ **[1]**

4. $\dfrac{1}{2} \times \dfrac{x}{5} \times \dfrac{x}{15} = 4$ **[1]**; $x^2 = 600$ **[1]**;
$x = \sqrt{600}$, $x = 10\sqrt{6}$ **[1]**

5. $x = \dfrac{7 \pm \sqrt{(-7)^2 - 4 \times 1 \times -15}}{2}$ **[1]**;
$x = -1.72$ and 8.72 (to 3 significant
figures) **[1]**

1. a) Correct curve **[1]**; correct straight
line **[1]**

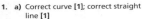
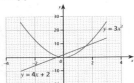

b) $x = 1.6$ to 1.8 **[1]**; (-0.3) to (-0.5) **[1]**
2. $y = x + 4$, $x + 4 = x^2 + 2$ **[1]**;
$x^2 - x - 2 = 0$ **[1]**; $(x - 2)(x + 1) = 0$,
$x = 2$, $y = 6$ **[1]**;
$x = -1$, $y = 3$ **[1]**

Page 41

1. a) $3n + 1$ **[1]**
b) $(3n + 1)(3(n + 1) + 1)$ **[1]**;
$9n^2 + 15n + 4$ **[1]**;
$3(3n^2 + 5n + 1) + 1$ **[1]**

2. $(n + 1)^2 - n^2$ **[1]**; $= n^2 + 2n + 1 - n^2$
$= 2n + 1$ **[1]**; $= n + (n + 1)$ **[1]**

3. $\dfrac{(x + 3)(x + 2)}{x^2 + 2x}$ **[1]**; $\dfrac{(x + 3)(x + 2)}{x(x + 2)}$ **[1]**;
$\dfrac{x + 3}{x}$ **[1]**

4. Any odd number -7 **[1]**

5. Area $= x^2$, diagonal $= \sqrt{x^2 + x^2}$
$= \sqrt{2x^2}$ **[1]**; $\sqrt{2x^2} \times \sqrt{2x^2} = 2x^2$,
$\dfrac{2x^2}{2} = x^2$ **[1]**

6. $9n^2 + 6n + 1 - (9n^2 - 6n + 1)$ **[1]**;
$12n$ **[1]**; $4(3n)$ **[1]**

7. a) $n^2 + 1$ **[1]**
b) $(n^2 + 1) + ((n + 1)^2 + 1)$ **[1]**;
$2n^2 + 2n + 3$ **[1]**; $2(n^2 + n + 1) + 1$ **[1]**

8. $\dfrac{2}{x - 2} - \dfrac{8}{(x + 2)(x - 2)}$ **[1]**; $\dfrac{2(x + 2)}{(x - 2)(x + 2)}$
$-\dfrac{8}{(x + 2)(x - 2)}$, $\dfrac{2x - 4}{(x + 2)(x - 2)}$ **[1]**;
$\dfrac{2(x - 2)}{(x + 2)(x - 2)}$, $\dfrac{2}{(x + 2)}$ **[1]**

9. $(2n + 1)^2$ **[1]** $= 4n^2 + 4n + 1$ **[1]**;
$4(n^2 + n) + 1$ **[1]**

10. The sum of any two primes that are
not 2, e.g. $3 + 5 = 8$ **[1]**

Circle Theorems 25/3/18   1-9

1.

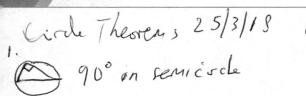

90° in semicircle

2. 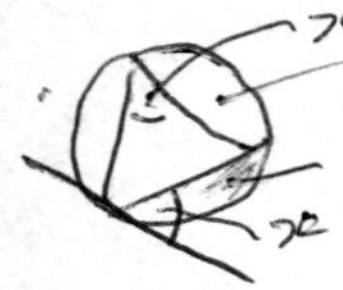   seg. B
     segment A   Alternate
                  segment .

3. 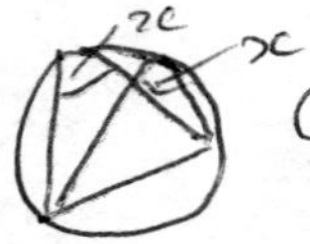   Corresponding △s
     are equal

4&5. 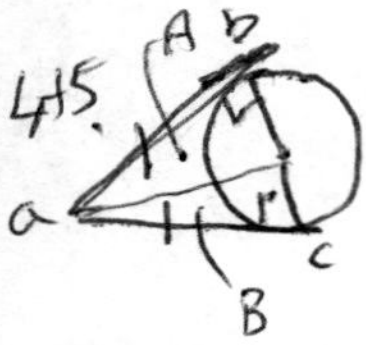 A I B = Congruent
      ab = ac

6.

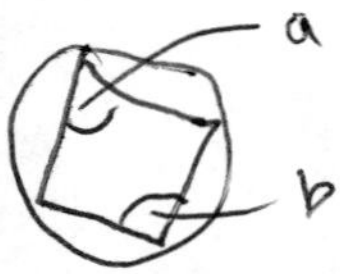

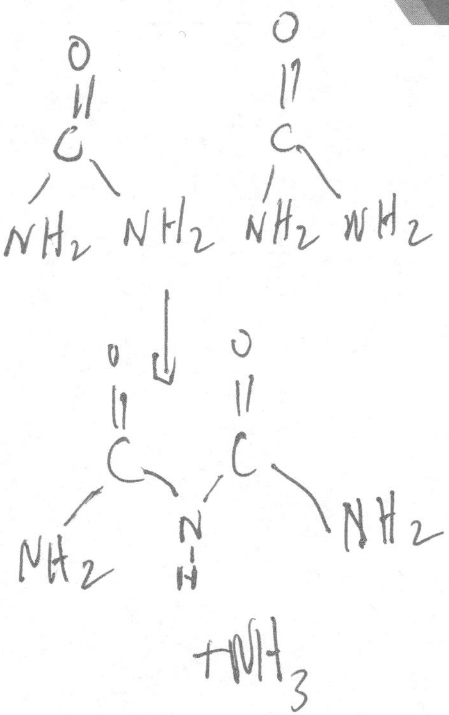

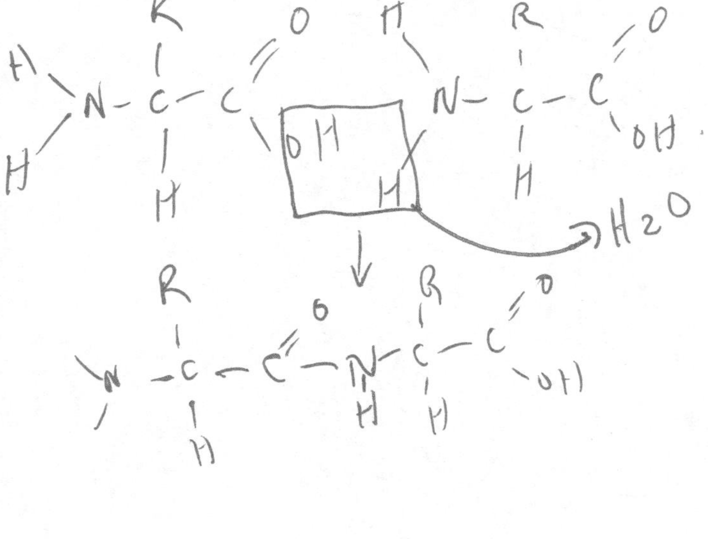

$$O$$
$$\|$$
$$C$$

$$O$$
$$\|$$
$$C$$

NH_2 NH_2 NH_2 NH_2

$$O$$
$$\|$$
$$C$$

$$O$$
$$\|$$
$$C$$

NH_2 N NH_2
       H

$+NH_3$

R   H   R   O
$H-N-C-C=O$ $N-C-C$
H C $\boxed{OH \quad H}$ OH
      H H

$\rightarrow H_2O$

R   O   R   O
$N-C-C=O-N-C-C=O$
H H H OH

Graph Paper